Weekend Treats

kids cook!

KIDS COOK SERIES

Copyright © Company's Coming Publishing Limited
All Rights Reserved
Second Printing July 2002

Canadian Cataloguing in Publication Data

Main entry under title:

Kids cook weekend treats

(Kids cook series)
Recipes selected from the Company's Coming cookbooks.
Includes index.
Co-published by The Recipe Factory Inc.
ISBN 1-896891-46-2

1. Cookery—Juvenile literature. I. Recipe Factory Inc.
II. Title: Weekend treats. III. Series.
TX652.5.K53 2000   j641.5'123   C00-900394-0

Published by
Company's Coming Publishing Limited
2311 - 96 Street
Edmonton, Alberta, Canada T6N 1G3
www.companyscoming.com

Printed In China

Table of Contents

Company's Coming Cookbooks

Original Series

- 150 Delicious Squares
- Casseroles
- Muffins & More
- Salads
- Appetizers
- Desserts
- Soups & Sandwiches
- Cookies
- Pasta
- Barbecues
- Light Recipes
- Preserves
- Chicken
- Kids Cooking
- Cooking For Two
- Breakfasts & Brunches
- Slow Cooker Recipes
- One-Dish Meals
- Starters
- Stir-Fry
- Make-Ahead Meals
- The Potato Book
- Low-Fat Cooking
- Low-Fat Pasta
- Cook For Kids
- Stews, Chilies & Chowders
- Fondues
- The Beef Book
- Asian Cooking
- The Cheese Book
- The Rookie Cook
- Rush-Hour Recipes
- Sweet Cravings ◄NEW► *November 1/02*

Greatest Hits Series

- Italian
- Mexican

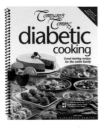

Lifestyle Series

- Grilling
- Diabetic Cooking

Special Occasion Series

- Gifts from the Kitchen
- Cooking for the Seasons
- Home for the Holidays ◄NEW► *October 1/02*

Foreword

Yeah—it's the weekend! You're hanging around the house and have an attack of the munchies. Your friends are coming over later and you'd like to serve some yummy snacks. Or, it's Dad's birthday and you've offered to make dessert. Whether you want something sweet or salty, something small or more substantial, you'll find it here. This collection of specially selected recipes from the Company's Coming family of cookbooks will help make your so-so weekend, a great weekend!

Before you get started, check out the Get Ready section of each recipe. Every utensil and piece of equipment you will need is listed in the order you will use it. Line them up as listed and you will have what you need when you need it! A picture dictionary of all the equipment and utensils can be found on pages 8 and 9. Any Cooking Terms you might not know are explained on pages 6 and 7.

And remember, there is always that one important last step. Clean up the kitchen when you're finished! It will make the weekend with your family and friends that much nicer.

Safety

1. Never touch anything electrical with your wet hands.
2. Always pull out a plug by holding and pulling on the plug itself, not the cord.
3. Keep saucepan handles turned inward on top of the stove.
4. Know how to properly use all appliances before starting. (Ask Mom or Dad if you're not sure.)
5. Handle hot plates and dishes with well-insulated oven mitts.
6. Turn off burners and oven, and unplug small appliances when not in use.

A note to parents: This book is intended for your children to use. It has been especially written for kids aged 8 to 15 years. Please supervise them when necessary. The handling of sharp knives, boiling liquids, and hot pans needs to be monitored carefully with younger children.

Cooking Terms

Bake
To cook in an oven preheated to the temperature it says in the recipe. Use either the bottom or center rack.

Batter
A mixture of flour, liquid and other ingredients that can be thin (such as pancake batter) or thick (such as muffin batter).

Beat
To mix two or more ingredients with a spoon, fork or electric mixer, using a circular motion.

Blend
To mix two or more ingredients with a spoon, fork, electric mixer, or electric blender until combined.

Boil
To heat a liquid in a saucepan until bubbles rise in a steady pattern and break on the surface. Steam also starts to rise from the surface.

Break An Egg
Tap the side of an egg on the edge of a bowl or cup to crack the shell. Place the tips of both thumbs in the crack and open the shell, letting the egg yolk and egg white drop into the bowl.

Broil
To cook under the top heating element in the oven. Use either the top rack or the upper rack.

Chill
To place in the refrigerator until cold.

Chop
To cut food into small pieces with a sharp knife on a cutting board; to chop finely is to cut foods as small as you can.

Combine
To put two or more ingredients together.

Cream
To beat an ingredient or combination of ingredients until the mixture is soft, smooth and "creamy," using a spoon or electric mixer.

Cut In
To combine butter or margarine with dry ingredients (such as flour) using a fork or pastry blender until the mixture looks like big crumbs the size of green peas.

Dice
To cut food into small 1/4 inch (6 mm) cube-shaped pieces.

Drain
To strain away an unwanted liquid (such as water, fruit juice, or grease) using a colander or strainer. Drain water or juice over the kitchen sink or in a bowl. Drain grease into a metal can, chill until hardened, then throw away in the garbage.

Drizzle
To dribble drops or lines of glaze or icing over food in a random manner from tines of a fork or the tip of a spoon.

Fold

To mix gently, using a rubber spatula, by cutting down in the center and lifting towards the edge of the bowl. Use a "down, up, over" movement, turning the bowl as you repeat.

Garnish

To decorate food with edible condiments such as parsley sprigs, fruit slices or vegetable cut-outs.

Heat

To make something warm or hot by placing the saucepan on the stove burner that is turned on to the level it says in the recipe.

Knead

To work dough into a smooth putty-like mass by pressing and folding using the heels of your hands.

Let Stand

To let a baked product cool slightly on a wire rack or hot pad, while still in its baking pan. Also, any other mixture that requires time to sit on the counter for the flavors to blend.

Mash

To squash cooked or very ripe foods with a fork or potato masher.

Melt

To heat a solid food such as butter, margarine, cheese or chocolate, until it turns into a liquid. Be careful not to burn it.

Mix

(see Combine)

Mixing Just Until Moistened

To stir dry ingredients with liquid ingredients until dry ingredients are barely wet. Mixture will still be lumpy.

Process

To mix or cut up food in a blender (or food processor) until it is the way it says in the recipe.

Sauté

To cook food quickly in a small amount of oil in a frying pan, wok, or special sauté pan over medium heat.

Scramble-Fry

To brown ground meat in hot oil using a spoon, fork or pancake lifter to break up the meat into small crumb-like pieces as it cooks.

Scrape (Scraping down the sides)

To use a rubber spatula to remove as much of a mixture as possible from inside a bowl or saucepan.

Simmer

To heat liquids in a saucepan on low on the stove burner so that small bubbles appear on the surface around the sides of the liquid.

Slice

To cut foods such as apples, carrots, tomatoes, meat or bread into thin sections or pieces, using a sharp knife.

Spoon (into)

Using a spoon to scoop ingredients from one container to another.

Spread

To cover the surface of one product (generally a more solid food such as bread) with another product (generally a softer food such as icing or butter).

Stir

To mix two or more ingredients with a spoon, using a circular motion.

Stir-Fry

To heat food quickly in a frying pan on medium-high stirring constantly.

Toast

To brown slightly in a toaster, frying pan or under the broiler in the oven.

Toss

To mix salad or other ingredients gently with a lifting motion, using two forks, two spoons or salad tongs.

Equipment & Utensils

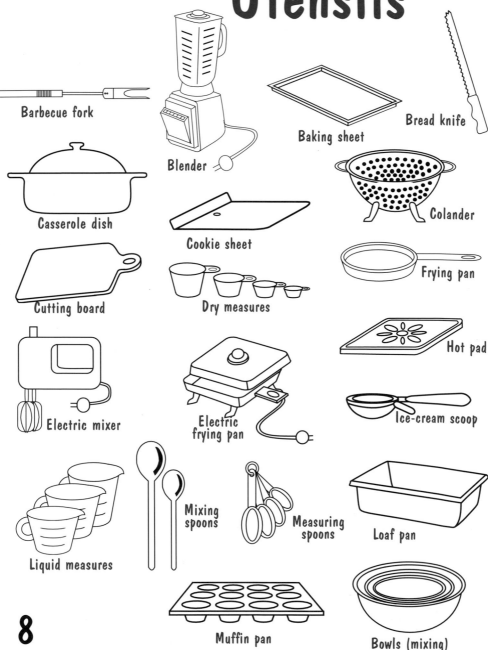

Barbecue fork

Blender

Baking sheet

Bread knife

Casserole dish

Cookie sheet

Colander

Cutting board

Dry measures

Frying pan

Electric mixer

Electric frying pan

Hot pad

Ice-cream scoop

Liquid measures

Mixing spoons

Measuring spoons

Loaf pan

Muffin pan

Bowls (mixing)

Oblong baking dish

Oblong baking pan

Oven mitts

Parfait spoon

Pancake lifter

Pastry brush

Pastry blender

Pie plate

Pizza pan

Rubber spatula

Rolling pin

Potato masher

Round cake pan

Square baking pan

Saucepan

Sharp knife

Table knife, fork & spoon

Tube pan

Sieve or strainer

Burners

Top Rack

Center Rack

Upper Rack

Bottom Rack

Wire rack

Tongs

Oven with rack positions

Whisk

9

Menu Suggestions

Slumber Party (for 6 kids)

Hot Tortilla Dip, page 41
Pita Pizza, page 47
Vanilla Milk Shake, page 14
Marshmallow Nests, page 65

Breakfast for the next morning
Pancakes, page 18

Birthday Party (for 8)

Rarebit Wieners, page 42
Nachos, page 44
Party Punch, page 13
Cone Cupcakes, page 62

Night At The Movies (for 5 or 6 kids)

Pizza Pop-Ups, page 48
Nacho Potato Chunks, page 49
Peanut Butter Candy, page 60
Popcorn Cake, page 63

Backyard Sleep Out (for 4 kids)

Surprise Dinner (for Mom & Dad)

Sunday Lunch (for Grandma & Grandpa)

Anniversary Breakfast In Bed (for Mom & Dad)

Mock Champagne

GET READY ✔
liquid measures, 2 quart (2 L) pitcher, long-handled mixing spoon, drinking glasses, sharp knife, cutting board

1.	White grape juice, chilled	4 cups	1 L
	Club soda, chilled	4 cups	1 L
2.	Ice cubes, per glass	2-3	2-3
	Lime (or lemon) slices, for garnish	10	10

1. Pour the white grape juice into the pitcher. Chill for about 2 hours. Immediately before serving, pour the club soda into the grape juice. Stir gently.

2. Place some ice cubes in each glass. Fill with the drink mixture. Cut the lime slice from the center through the outside of the peel on the cutting board. Fit over the edge of each glass. Makes about 7½ cups (1.9 L).

A fine-tasting bubbly drink, almost like the real thing!
Do not freeze.

A smooth fruit punch. Do not freeze.

Party Punch

GET READY ✔
2 quart (2 L) pitcher (or small punch bowl), liquid measures, long-handled mixing spoon, drinking glasses (or punch cups)

1.	Frozen concentrated orange juice, thawed	½ x 12½ oz.	½ x 355 mL
	Frozen concentrated lemonade, thawed	½ x 12½ oz.	½ x 355 mL
	Pineapple juice	2 cups	500 mL
2.	Ginger ale	4 cups	1 L
3.	Ice cubes, per glass	2-3	2-3
	Maraschino cherries, for garnish	10	10
	Orange slices, for garnish	10	10

1. Empty the concentrated orange juice and lemonade into the pitcher. Add the pineapple juice. Stir well. Chill until ready to serve.

2. Add the ginger ale to the juice mixture. Stir gently. If using a punch bowl, empty the juices from the pitcher into the bowl. Add the ginger ale. Stir gently.

3. Put 2 or 3 ice cubes into each glass or punch cup. Fill with the punch. Makes 7½ cups (1.9 L).

Vanilla Milk Shake

GET READY ✔

ice-cream scoop, liquid measures, measuring spoons, blender, drinking glass, drinking straw

1.			
Rounded scoops of vanilla ice cream	2	2
Milk	³⁄₄ cup	175 mL
Instant vanilla pudding powder	1 tbsp.	15 mL
Vanilla flavoring	½ tsp.	2 mL

1. Place all 4 ingredients in the blender. Place the lid on the blender. Process the ice cream mixture for about 20 seconds until smooth and frothy. Serve in the glass with the straw. Makes about 2 cups (500 mL).

CHOCOLATE MILK SHAKE: Leave out the vanilla flavoring. Add 2 tbsp. (30 mL) chocolate syrup.

STRAWBERRY MILK SHAKE: Leave out the vanilla flavoring. Increase the milk to 1 cup (250 mL) and add ½ cup (125 mL) sliced strawberries. Strawberry ice cream can also be used instead of the vanilla ice cream.

ORANGE MILK SHAKE: Leave out the vanilla flavoring and milk. Add 1 cup (250 mL) orange soft drink.

CHOCO BANANA MILK SHAKE: Leave out the vanilla flavoring. Add 2 tbsp. (30 mL) chocolate syrup and 1 ripe banana, sliced.

PURPLE COW: Leave out the vanilla flavoring. Add ½ cup (125 mL) grape soft drink.

1. Strawberry Milk Shake
2. Orange Milk Shake
3. Choco Banana Milk Shake
4. Purple Cow
5. Vanilla Milk Shake
6. Chocolate Milk Shake

Hot Cocoa

GET READY ✔
measuring spoons, mug that holds 1 cup (250 mL), small mixing spoon, liquid measures, small saucepan

1.	Cocoa powder	1½ tsp.	7 mL
	Granulated sugar	1½ tsp.	7 mL
	Water	1½ tsp.	7 mL
2.	Milk	¾ cup	175 mL
3.	Miniature marshmallows (or frozen whipped topping)	3-4	3-4

1. Mix the cocoa powder, sugar and water in the mug until smooth.

2. Pour the milk into the saucepan. Heat on medium, stirring slowly to make sure it does not burn, until steaming. Carefully pour the milk into the mug. Stir.

3. Top with the marshmallows. Serves 1.

Easy to make for yourself but you can also make it for your friends.

A picturesque way to serve
eggs. Do not freeze.

Framed Eggs

GET READY ✔
frying pan with lid, measuring spoons, table knife, drinking glass, pancake lifter,
large plate

1.	Margarine	2 tsp.	10 mL
	White (or whole wheat) bread slice	1	1
	(1 inch, 2.5 cm, thick)		
2.	Margarine	½ tsp.	2 mL
	Large egg	1	1
	Salt, sprinkle		
	Pepper, sprinkle		

1.   Heat the frying pan on medium. Spread the first amount of margarine on both
     sides of the bread slice with the table knife. Place the drinking glass upside down
     on the center of the bread slice. Press to cut out a round piece. Place both the
     bread slice and round piece of bread in the frying pan. Brown 1 side of each.
     Turn the heat to medium-low. Use the pancake lifter to turn both pieces over.

2.   Melt the second amount of margarine in the hole in the bread slice. Break the
     egg into the hole. Sprinkle with the salt and pepper. Place the lid on the frying
     pan. Cook slowly until the white of the egg is set. Remove the lid. Remove the
     egg and toast with the lifter to the plate. Garnish with the toasted round piece.
     Serves 1.

Start the day right or even enjoy these for lunch or supper. For fun, try a creative design such as your initials.

Pancakes

GET READY ✔

small bowl, mixing spoon, liquid measures, measuring spoons, dry measures, no-stick cooking spray, large table spoon, frying pan, pancake lifter, large plate

1.	Large eggs	2	2
2.	Milk	1 cup	250 mL
	Cooking oil	2 tbsp.	30 mL
3.	All-purpose flour	1¼ cups	300 mL
	Granulated sugar	1 tbsp.	15 mL
	Baking powder	1 tbsp.	15 mL
	Salt	¼ tsp.	1 mL

1. Break the eggs into the bowl. Stir until the eggs are fairly smooth and a bit bubbly.

2. Add the milk and cooking oil. Mix.

3. Add the remaining 4 ingredients. Stir just until moistened. Heat the frying pan until a few drops of water bounce all over. Spray with the no-stick cooking spray. Scoop spoonfuls of the batter into the frying pan using the large table spoon. When the tops are bubbly and the edges are a bit dry, turn over with the pancake lifter to brown the other side. Remove with the lifter to the plate. Repeat until all the batter is used. Makes 18 round pancakes.

French Toast

GET READY ✔
9 inch (22 cm) pie plate, table fork, measuring spoons, frying pan, pancake lifter, large plate, table spoon, sieve

1. **Large egg**	**1**	**1**
Milk (or water)	**3 tbsp.**	**50 mL**
Salt	**⅛ tsp.**	**0.5 mL**
Vanilla flavoring	**⅛ tsp.**	**0.5 mL**
2. **Margarine**	**2 tsp.**	**10 mL**
3. **French bread slices, cut 1 inch** **(2.5 cm) thick**	**2-3**	**2-3**
4. **Icing (confectioner's) sugar, sprinkle**		

1. Break the egg into the pie plate. Beat with the fork. Add the milk, salt and vanilla flavoring. Beat with the fork to mix.

2. Melt the margarine in the frying pan on medium.

3. Dip the bread slices, 1 at a time, into the egg mixture, turning to coat both sides. Place the slices in the frying pan. Brown 1 side. Use the pancake lifter to turn the slices over. Brown the other side. Use the lifter to remove the slices to the large plate.

4. Put a spoonful of the icing sugar into the sieve. Shake it gently over top of the slices to give a light sprinkle. Serves 2.

**Serve with maple syrup.
A scrumptious breakfast.**

Great! Lots of cheese.

Easy Oven Omelet

GET READY ✔

deep 9 inch (22 cm) pie plate (or 1 quart, 1 L, casserole dish), measuring spoons, medium bowl, electric mixer, dry measures, table knife, oven mitts, wire rack

1.	Large eggs	6	6
	Can of skim evaporated milk	13½ oz.	385 mL
	All-purpose flour	1 tbsp.	15 mL
	Salt	¼ tsp.	1 mL
2.	Grated Cheddar (or Swiss) cheese	1½ cups	375 mL
	Green onions, sliced	2	2
	Medium tomato, chopped	1	1

1. Place the oven rack in the center position. Turn the oven on to 325°F (160°C). Grease the pie plate. Put the eggs, evaporated milk, flour and salt into the bowl. Beat on medium with the mixer.

2. Scatter the remaining 3 ingredients in the bottom of the pie plate. Pour the egg mixture carefully over top. Bake in the oven for 60 to 65 minutes until the knife inserted in the center of the omelet comes out clean. Use the oven mitts to remove the pie plate to the wire rack. Serves 4.

Fruit Waffles À La Mode

GET READY ✓
baking sheet, table spoon, liquid measures, oven mitts, wire rack, pancake lifter, medium plates, ice-cream scoop

1.	Frozen plain (or buttermilk) waffles	2	2
2.	Canned cherry pie filling	½ cup	125 mL
3.	Small scoops of vanilla ice cream	2	2
	Maraschino cherries, with stems	2	2

1. Place the oven rack in the center position. Turn the oven on to 350°F (175°C). Place both waffles on the ungreased baking sheet.

2. Spoon ¼ cup (60 mL) of the pie filling onto each waffle. Bake in the oven for 20 minutes until the pie filling is hot and bubbling and the waffle is crisp. Use the oven mitts to remove the baking sheet to the wire rack. Use the pancake lifter to place the waffles on the plates.

3. Top each hot waffle with 1 scoop of the ice cream. Top each scoop with a maraschino cherry. Makes 2 waffles.

As delicious as cherry pie. Use a variety of pie fillings for different tastes. Try peach or raisin. Gets top marks for presentation and eye appeal.

Crispy Fruit Pizza

GET READY ✔
dry measures, large saucepan, 3 mixing spoons, hot pad, 12 inch (30 cm) pizza pan, small bowl, electric mixer, rubber spatula, measuring spoons, small cup, pastry brush, liquid measures, medium bowl, table spoon

1.	**CRUST**		
	Hard margarine	¼ cup	60 mL
	Large marshmallows	32	32
2.	Crisp rice cereal	5 cups	1.25 L
3.	**TOPPING**		
	Cream cheese, softened	8 oz.	250 g
	Icing (confectioner's) sugar	2 cups	500 mL
	Cocoa powder	¼ cup	60 mL
4.	Small strawberries, halved	16	16
	Banana, sliced	1	1
	Kiwifruit, halved lengthwise and sliced	2	2
5.	**GLAZE**		
	Apricot jam	2 tbsp.	30 mL
	Water	1½ tsp.	7 mL
6.	Envelope of dessert topping (not prepared)	1	1
	Milk	⅔ cup	150 mL
	Vanilla flavoring	½ tsp.	2 mL

1. **Crust:** Combine the margarine and marshmallows in the saucepan. Heat on medium-low, stirring often, until melted.

2. Remove the saucepan to the hot pad. Add the cereal. Stir until the cereal is well coated. Grease the pizza pan. Press the cereal mixture evenly in the pan with your wet fingers. Cool.

3. **Topping:** Put the cream cheese, icing sugar and cocoa powder into the small bowl. Use the mixer to beat on low just until moistened. Beat on medium until smooth. Spread over the cooled pizza crust with the rubber spatula.

4. Arrange the strawberries, banana and kiwifruit over the chocolate topping in a fancy design.

5. **Glaze:** Mix the
    jam and water in
    the cup. Use the pastry
    brush to dab the fruit with the
    jam mixture. The glaze will prevent
    the fruit from turning brown.

6. Beat the dessert topping, milk and vanilla flavoring in the medium bowl until
    thickened. Dab on top of the pizza. Cuts into 8 to 10 wedges.

Dark Blue Heaven Dessert

GET READY ✔
9 x 13 inch (22 x 33 cm) oblong baking pan, small mixing spoon, rubber spatula, measuring spoons, small cup, dry measures, wooden toothpick, oven mitts, wire rack

1.	Can of crushed pineapple, with juice	19 oz.	540 mL
	Can of blueberry pie filling	19 oz.	540 mL
	Yellow cake mix (2 layer size)	1	1
2.	Granulated sugar	1 tbsp.	15 mL
	Ground cinnamon	½ tsp.	2 mL
3.	Hard margarine, thinly sliced	1 cup	250 mL
	Chopped walnuts	¾ cup	175 mL

1. Place the oven rack in the center position. Turn the oven on to 350°F (175°C). Grease the pan. Spread the pineapple with juice in the pan. Drop small spoonfuls of the pie filling here and there over the pineapple. Use the spatula to empty the can. Sprinkle the dry cake mix evenly over the pie filling.

2. Mix the sugar and cinnamon in the small cup. Sprinkle evenly over the cake mix.

3. Arrange the margarine slices over the top of the cake mix. Sprinkle with the walnuts. Bake in the oven for 45 to 55 minutes. The wooden toothpick inserted in the center of the cake should come out clean. Use the oven mitts to remove the pan to the wire rack. Cuts into 15 pieces.

This easy dessert looks as delicious as it tastes. Serve in squares, warm with ice cream, or cold with whipped cream or ice cream.

Raisin Cobbler

GET READY ✔
1½ quart (1.5 L) casserole dish, measuring spoons, 2 mixing spoons, medium bowl, liquid measures, dry measures, oven mitts, wire rack, wooden toothpick

1.	Can of raisin pie filling	19 oz.	540 mL
	Lemon juice	1 tsp.	5 mL
2.	Large egg	1	1
	Cooking oil	⅓ cup	75 mL
	Milk	⅓ cup	75 mL
3.	All-purpose flour	1½ cups	375 mL
	Granulated sugar	⅓ cup	75 mL
	Baking powder	2 tsp.	10 mL
	Salt	½ tsp.	2 mL

1. Place the oven rack in the center position. Turn the oven on to 400°F (205°C). Pour the raisin pie filling into the ungreased casserole dish. Add the lemon juice. Stir into the filling. Place the casserole, uncovered, in the oven to heat while preparing the topping.

2. Break the egg into the bowl. Use the spoon to beat until fairly smooth. Add the cooking oil and milk to the egg. Stir.

3. Add the flour, sugar, baking powder and salt. Stir just until moistened. Use the oven mitts to remove the casserole dish to the wire rack. Drop the batter by rounded tablespoonfuls over top of the filling. Return the casserole dish to the oven. Bake, uncovered, in the oven for 20 to 25 minutes. The wooden toothpick inserted in the center of the topping should come out clean. Use the oven mitts to remove the casserole dish to the wire rack. Serve warm. Serves 6.

If your favorite filling is blueberry or cherry, use it rather than the raisin. Good and easy.

Desserts 25

Tomato Soup Cake

GET READY ✔
9 × 9 inch (22 × 22 cm) square baking pan, measuring spoons, dry measures, large bowl, electric mixer, rubber spatula, mixing spoon, wooden toothpick, oven mitts, wire rack

1.	Hard margarine, softened	6 tbsp.	100 mL
	Condensed tomato soup	10 oz.	284 mL
	All-purpose flour	1½ cups	375 mL
	Granulated sugar	1 cup	250 mL
	Large egg	1	1
	Baking soda	1 tsp.	5 mL
	Ground cinnamon	1 tsp.	5 mL
	Ground allspice	¼ tsp.	1 mL
	Salt	¼ tsp.	1 mL
2.	Raisins (optional)	¾ cup	175 mL
	Cream Cheese Icing, page 27		

1. Place the oven rack in the center position. Turn the oven on to 350°F (175°C). Grease the inside of the pan. Measure the first 9 ingredients into the bowl. Use the mixer to beat on low until the flour is just moistened. Beat on medium, scraping down the sides of the bowl 2 or 3 times with the rubber spatula, until the batter is smooth.

2. Add the raisins. Stir to distribute them. Turn the batter into the pan. Bake in the oven for about 35 minutes. The wooden toothpick inserted in the center of the cake should come out clean. Use the oven mitts to remove the pan to the wire rack. Cool. Ice. Makes 1 cake.

Pictured on page 27.

Tomato Soup Cake, page 26, is an old-fashioned cake that is prepared in one bowl. The Cream Cheese Icing makes this cake really yummy.

Cream Cheese Icing

GET READY ✔
measuring spoons, dry measures, medium bowl, electric mixer, table knife

1.			
Cream cheese, softened	4 oz.	125 g
Hard margarine, softened	2 tbsp.	30 mL
Icing (confectioner's) sugar	1½ cups	375 mL
Vanilla flavoring	½ tsp.	2 mL

1. Combine the cream cheese, margarine, icing sugar and vanilla flavoring in the bowl. Use the mixer to beat on low just until moistened. Beat on medium until smooth and fluffy. Spread over Tomato Soup Cake, page 26. Makes 1¼ cups (300 mL), enough to ice a 9 x 9 inch (22 x 22 cm) cake.

Grilled Cheese Sandwich

GET READY ✔

frying pan, measuring spoons, table knife, pancake lifter, small plate, sharp knife

1. | Margarine | 2 tsp. | 10 mL |
   |---|---|---|
   | White (or whole wheat) bread slices | 2 | 2 |
   | Yellow cheese slice | 1 | 1 |

1. Heat the frying pan on medium-high. Spread the margarine on 1 side of both bread slices. Place 1 slice, buttered side down, in the frying pan. Place the cheese slice on top. Cover with the second bread slice, buttered side up. When the bottom side is browned, use the pancake lifter to turn the sandwich over. Brown the other side. Use the lifter to remove the sandwich to the plate. Cut in half. Makes 1 sandwich.

   Pictured on page 29.

Meaty Buns

GET READY ✔

dry measures, measuring spoons, medium bowl, mixing spoon, table knife, baking sheet, oven mitts, wire rack, pancake lifter, plate

1. | Can of processed meat, mashed | 12 oz. | 340 g |
   |---|---|---|
   | Grated Cheddar cheese | 2 cups | 500 mL |
   | Finely chopped green pepper | ½ cup | 125 mL |
   | Condensed tomato soup | 10 oz. | 284 mL |
   | Worcestershire sauce | 2 tsp. | 10 mL |
   | Sweet pickle relish | 2 tbsp. | 30 mL |
   | Onion salt | ½ tsp. | 2 mL |
   | Hamburger buns, split in half | 8 | 8 |

1. Place the oven rack in the top position. Turn the oven on to broil. Combine the first 7 ingredients in the bowl. Mix well. Makes 4 cups (1 L) filling. Divide the mixture among the bun halves. Spread to the edges. Place on the ungreased baking sheet. Broil to melt the cheese. Use the oven mitts to remove the baking sheet to the wire rack. Use the pancake lifter to remove the buns to the plate. Makes 16 bun halves.

   Pictured on page 29.

Scrambled Egg Sandwich

GET READY ✔
cutting board, measuring spoons, table knife, table fork, small bowl, frying pan, long-handled mixing spoon, sharp knife, cutting board, pancake lifter, small plate

1.	White (or whole wheat) bread slices	2	2
	Margarine	2 tsp.	10 mL
2.	Large egg	1	1
	Water	1 tbsp.	15 mL
	Margarine	½ tsp.	2 mL
3.	Salt, sprinkle (optional)		
	Pepper, sprinkle (optional)		
	Ketchup	2 tsp.	10 mL

1. Place the bread slices on the cutting board. Spread the first amount of margarine on 1 side of both bread slices.

2. Mix the egg and water with the fork in the bowl. Melt the second amount of margarine in the frying pan on medium. Add the egg mixture. Stir constantly until cooked.

3. Spread the cooked egg mixture on the buttered side of 1 slice of bread. Sprinkle with the salt and pepper. Spread the ketchup on the buttered side of the second slice of bread. Place the second slice over the top of the egg mixture, unbuttered side up. Cut in half on the cutting board. Use the pancake lifter to transfer the sandwich to the plate. Makes 1 sandwich.

This Scrambled Egg Sandwich, pictured at top right, is quick to prepare for lunch or a snack. Do not freeze. Shown on the left, the Grilled Cheese Sandwich goes great with a bowl of hot soup. Use your favorite canned meat to make Meaty Buns, shown at the bottom.

Fried Onion Dogs

GET READY ✓

measuring spoons, frying pan, long-handled mixing spoon, hot pad, table spoon

1.	Margarine	2 tsp.	10 mL
	Small onion, cut into thin rings	1	1
	Wieners, cut into thin slices	2	2
2.	Hot dog buns, split open	2	2
	Condiments (such as prepared mustard, ketchup and sweet pickle relish), optional		

1. Melt the margarine in the frying pan on medium. Add the onion rings. Sauté for 3 minutes, stirring often, until the onion is soft. Add the wiener slices. Turn down the heat to low. Sauté, stirring occasionally, for about 6 minutes until the onion is golden. Remove the frying pan to the hot pad.

2. Spoon the mixture on the buns. Top with the mustard, ketchup and relish. Makes 2 onion dogs.

The onion really mellows and "sweetens" when cooked.

Make this delicious homemade version.

Creamy Macaroni & Cheese

GET READY ✓
measuring spoons, small saucepan, dry measures, 2 mixing spoons, liquid measures, hot pad, large saucepan, colander

1.	**Margarine**	1 tbsp.	15 mL
	Chopped onion	¼ cup	60 mL
2.	**All-purpose flour**	1½ tbsp.	25 mL
	Skim evaporated milk	1 cup	250 mL
	Grated Cheddar cheese	½ cup	125 mL
	Process Cheddar cheese slices	2	2
	Salt	¼ tsp.	1 mL
	Pepper, sprinkle		
	Dry mustard (or paprika)	¾ tsp.	4 mL
3.	**Water**	8 cups	2 L
	Elbow macaroni (or small shell pasta), uncooked	1 cup	250 mL

1. Melt the margarine in the small saucepan on medium. Sauté the onion until soft.

2. Stir in the flour. Gradually add the evaporated milk, stirring constantly, until boiling. Stir in both cheeses, salt, pepper and mustard. Stir until the cheeses are melted. Remove from the heat to the hot pad.

3. Measure the water into the large saucepan. Bring to a boil. Stir in the macaroni. Cook for 5 to 6 minutes until the macaroni is just tender. Drain in the colander. Return the macaroni to the saucepan. Add the cheese sauce. Stir well. Makes 4 cups (1 L).

Snappy Lunch

GET READY ✔
liquid measures, microwave-safe cereal bowl, measuring spoons, mixing spoon, oven mitts, hot pad

1.	**Canned kidney beans**	**½ cup**	**125 mL**
	Salsa	**3 tbsp.**	**50 mL**
2.	**Grated Cheddar cheese**	**2 tbsp.**	**30 mL**
	Grated mozzarella cheese	**2 tbsp.**	**30 mL**

1. Put the kidney beans into the bowl. Add the salsa. Stir.

2. Sprinkle with both cheeses. Microwave on high (100%) for about 2 minutes until the cheeses are melted. Use the oven mitts to remove the bowl to the hot pad. Serves 1.

An exceptionally good quick meal.

A very different taco. Most enjoyable. Do not freeze.

Tacos

GET READY ✔
non-stick frying pan, measuring spoons, dry measures, 5 small bowls

1.	**Frozen breaded fish sticks**	**2**	**2**
2.	**Taco (or seafood) sauce**	**1 tbsp.**	**15 mL**
	Chopped iceberg lettuce	**¼ cup**	**60 mL**
	Tomato slice, diced	**1**	**1**
	Grated Cheddar cheese	**2 tbsp.**	**30 mL**
	Sour cream (optional)	**1 tbsp.**	**15 mL**
3.	**Taco shells**	**2**	**2**

1. Heat the fish sticks in the frying pan on medium.

2. Prepare and measure the next 5 ingredients into separate small bowls.

3. Place a fish stick in each taco shell. Layer the taco sauce, lettuce, tomato, cheese and sour cream over each fish stick. Makes 2 tacos.

Mexican Stir-Fry Sandwich

GET READY ✔

measuring spoons, frying pan, long-handled mixing spoon, dry measures, hot pad

1.	Cooking oil	1 tsp.	5 mL
	Boneless, skinless chicken breast half, slivered	1	1
2.	Garlic powder	⅛ tsp.	0.5 mL
	Salt	⅛ tsp.	0.5 mL
	Pepper	1/16 tsp.	0.5 mL
3.	Small red onion, thinly sliced	½	½
	Medium green pepper, slivered	1	1
	Salsa	⅓ cup	75 mL
4.	White (or whole wheat) flour tortillas (10 inch, 25 cm, size)	3	3

Use medium or hot salsa if you want to make these spicier.

1. Heat the cooking oil in the frying pan on medium-high. Add the chicken. Stir-fry for 2 minutes.

2. Add the garlic powder, salt and pepper. Stir-fry for 2 minutes.

3. Add the red onion and green pepper to the chicken. Stir-fry for 3 minutes. Add the salsa. Stir-fry for 2 minutes until the vegetables are tender-crisp. Remove the frying pan to the hot pad. Makes 2 cups (500 mL) filling.

4. Divide the filling evenly among the tortillas. To roll, fold the bottom edge of the tortilla up over the chicken mixture to the center. Fold the left side over the center. Fold the right side overlapping the left side. Makes 3 rolled sandwiches.

Serve over toast,
toasted bun halves, or
inside slightly
hollowed-out buns.

Easy Chili

GET READY ✔

non-stick frying pan with lid, long-handled mixing spoon, measuring spoons

1.	Lean ground beef	1 lb.	454 g
	Medium onion, chopped	1	1
	Large celery rib, sliced	1	1
2.	All-purpose flour	2 tbsp.	30 mL
	Can of stewed tomatoes, with juice, chopped	14 oz.	398 mL
	Garlic powder	¼ tsp.	1 mL
	Can of kidney beans, drained	14 oz.	398 mL
	Chili powder	1 tbsp.	15 mL
	Granulated sugar	2 tsp.	10 mL
	Paprika	1 tsp.	5 mL
	Salt	½ tsp.	2 mL

1. Scramble-fry the ground beef, onion and celery in the frying pan on medium until the beef is no longer pink and the vegetables are tender-crisp.

2. Sprinkle the surface of the beef mixture with the flour. Stir for 1 minute. Add the remaining 7 ingredients. Bring to a boil. Place the lid on the frying pan. Simmer on low for 30 minutes, stirring several times. Makes 5¾ cups (1.45 L).

Chicken Pasta Casserole

GET READY ✔
liquid measures, dry measures, measuring spoons, large bowl, mixing spoon, 3 quart (3 L) casserole dish, oven mitts, wire rack

1.			
Condensed cream of mushroom soup	10 oz.	284 mL
Condensed cream of celery soup	10 oz.	284 mL
Water	2½ cups	625 mL
Grated Cheddar cheese	2 cups	500 mL
Diced cooked chicken (see Note)	2 cups	500 mL
Macaroni, uncooked	2 cups	500 mL
Diced onion	1 cup	250 mL
Salt	1 tsp.	5 mL
2. Shoestring potato chips	1 cup	250 mL

1. Mix the first 8 ingredients in the bowl. Turn into the ungreased casserole dish. Cover with the lid. Chill overnight.

2. Place the oven rack in the center position. Turn the oven on to 350°F (175°C). Take the casserole dish from the refrigerator. Remove the lid. Sprinkle the potato chips over the top. Bake, uncovered, for 1 hour until the pasta is tender. Use the oven mitts to remove the casserole dish to the wire rack. Serves 6.

Note: If you don't have cooked chicken on hand, use two 6½ oz. (184 g) cans of flaked or chunk chicken, drained.

Make this the night before. Then all you have to do is put it into the oven the next day. The pasta is not precooked.

Ten of the juiciest meat servings ever. Just the right size to freeze. They are thin enough to thaw quickly.

Little Meat Muffins

GET READY ✔
medium bowl, mixing spoon, muffin pan (for 10 muffins), baking sheet, oven mitts, wire rack

| 1. | Lean ground beef | 1 lb. | 454 g |
| | Condensed vegetable soup | 10 oz. | 284 mL |

1. Place the oven rack in the center position. Turn the oven on to 350°F (175°C). Mix the ground beef and soup in the bowl. Pack the beef mixture into 10 greased muffin cups. Set the muffin pan on the baking sheet to catch any drips. Bake for 40 to 45 minutes. Use the oven mitts to remove the muffin pan to the wire rack. Let stand for 10 minutes before serving. Makes 10 meat muffins.

Chops are cooked with a dark sauce.

Pork Chops

GET READY ✔
measuring spoons, frying pan, pancake lifter, table fork, small roasting pan, dry measures, small bowl, mixing spoon, oven mitts, hot pad

1.	**Cooking oil**	**1 tbsp.**	**15 mL**
	Pork chops, trimmed of fat	**6**	**6**
2.	**Chopped onion**	**1 cup**	**250 mL**
3.	**Ketchup**	**½ cup**	**125 mL**
	Brown sugar, packed	**¼ cup**	**60 mL**
	White vinegar	**3 tbsp.**	**50 mL**
	Soy sauce	**1 tbsp.**	**15 mL**
	Salt	**½ tsp.**	**2 mL**
	Pepper	**⅛ tsp.**	**0.5 mL**

1. Place the oven rack in the center position. Turn the oven on to 350°F (175°C). Heat the cooking oil in the frying pan on medium. Add the pork chops. Brown 1 side. Use the pancake lifter to turn the chops over. Brown. Use the fork to transfer the chops to the roasting pan.

2. Scatter the onion over the chops.

3. Measure the remaining 6 ingredients into the bowl. Stir. Pour over the chops and onion. Place the lid on the roasting pan. Bake for about 1 hour until the meat is tender. Use the oven mitts to remove the roasting pan to the hot pad. Serves 6.

Stroganoff

GET READY ✔
measuring spoons, frying pan with lid, long-handled mixing spoon, liquid measures, dry measures

1.	**Cooking oil**	**1 tbsp.**	**15 mL**
	Lean ground beef	**1 lb.**	**454 g**
2.	**Condensed cream of mushroom soup**	**10 oz.**	**284 mL**
	Water	**1 cup**	**250 mL**
	Envelope of dry onion soup mix	**1¼ oz.**	**38 g**
	Medium noodles, uncooked	**1 cup**	**250 mL**
	Can of sliced mushrooms, drained	**10 oz.**	**284 mL**
	Ketchup	**1 tbsp.**	**15 mL**
3.	**Sour cream**	**½ cup**	**125 mL**
	Yellow cheese slice, broken up	**1**	**1**

1. Heat the cooking oil in the frying pan on medium. Add the ground beef. Scramble-fry until the meat is browned and crumbly.

2. Add the next 6 ingredients to the beef. Stir. Place the lid on the frying pan. Simmer on low for about 10 minutes until the pasta is tender but firm. Remove the lid.

3. Add the sour cream and cheese. Stir until the cheese melts. Serves 4.

Add a salad and a vegetable and you're all set. The pasta is added raw.

These might look like cinnamon rolls, but they have a great pizza flavor.

Pizza Pinwheels

GET READY ✔

baking sheet, dry measures, liquid measures, medium bowl, mixing spoon, rolling pin, ruler, measuring spoons, small bowl, sharp knife, cutting board, oven mitts, wire rack

1.	**Biscuit mix**	**2¼ cups**	**560 mL**
	Water	**½ cup**	**125 mL**
	Biscuit mix, as needed, to prevent sticking		
2.	**Pizza sauce**	**7½ oz.**	**213 mL**
	Green onions, sliced	**2**	**2**
	Finely chopped green pepper	**½ cup**	**125 mL**
	Finely chopped pepperoni	**½ cup**	**125 mL**
	Grated mozzarella cheese	**1 cup**	**250 mL**
	Dried whole oregano	**¼ tsp.**	**1 mL**

1. Place the oven rack in the center position. Turn the oven on to 400°F (205°C). Grease the baking sheet. Stir the biscuit mix and water in the medium bowl until the dough starts to form a ball. Turn the dough out onto the counter that has been lightly dusted with more biscuit mix. Gently knead the dough 20 times. Dust the dough with the biscuit mix and roll out to a 12 x 12 inch (30 x 30 cm) square.

2. Combine the remaining 6 ingredients in the small bowl. Mix well. Spread over the dough, leaving about 1 inch (2.5 cm) all around the outside edge. Roll up the dough from 1 side to the other like a jelly roll. Pinch along the long edge of the roll to seal. Cut into twelve 1 inch (2.5 cm) thick slices on the cutting board. Place the slices on the baking sheet. Bake in the oven for 12 minutes. Use the oven mitts to remove the baking sheet to the wire rack. Makes 12 pinwheels.

Hot Tortilla Dip

GET READY ✔
dry measures, small microwave-safe bowl, sharp knife, cutting board, paper towel, mixing spoon, measuring spoons, plastic wrap, oven mitts, hot pad

1.	Chunky salsa	½ cup	125 mL
	Small tomato	1	1
2.	Green onion, thinly sliced	1	1
	Dried crushed chilies	⅛ tsp.	0.5 mL
3.	Process cheese loaf (such as Velveeta), cut into small cubes	4 oz.	125 g

1. Measure the salsa into the bowl. Cut the tomato in half on the cutting board. Gently squeeze the tomato over the paper towel to remove the seeds. Discard the seeds and juice. Dice the tomato into small pieces on the cutting board. Stir into the salsa.

2. Add the green onion and crushed chilies. Cover loosely with plastic wrap. Microwave on high (100%) for 1 minute.

3. Stir the cheese into the warm salsa mixture. Microwave, uncovered, on high (100%) for 30 seconds. Stir well. Repeat until the cheese is melted. Use the oven mitts to remove the bowl to the hot pad. Makes 1¼ cups (300 mL).

Make this ahead and keep chilled. Reheat for lunch!

Rarebit Wieners

GET READY ✔
baking sheet, dry measures, measuring spoons, small bowl, mixing spoon, table knife, oven mitts, wire rack

1.	Hamburger buns, split and lightly toasted	2	2
2.	Wieners, sliced	2	2
	Grated Cheddar cheese	½ cup	125 mL
	Dry mustard	½ tsp.	2 mL
	Ketchup	1 tbsp.	15 mL
	Salad dressing (or mayonnaise)	1 tbsp.	15 mL
3.	Paprika, sprinkle		

Lots of hot dog taste!

1. Place the oven rack in the center position. Turn the oven on to 350°F (175°C). Place the bun halves, toasted side up, on the ungreased baking sheet.

2. Mix the next 5 ingredients in the bowl. Divide the mixture among the 4 bun halves. Pack down with the table knife to cover to the edge of the buns.

3. Sprinkle lightly with the paprika. Bake in the oven for 15 minutes until the tops are bubbly and starting to brown. Use the oven mitts to remove the baking sheet to the wire rack. Makes 4 bun halves.

Great dip for nacho chips, veggies or bread. Just like a fondue.

Hot Mushroom Cheddar Dip

GET READY ✔
liquid measures, dry measures, measuring spoons, medium microwave-safe bowl, mixing spoon

1.			
Condensed cream of mushroom soup	10 oz.	284 mL
Skim evaporated milk	¾ cup	175 mL
Grated Cheddar cheese	2 cups	500 mL
Worcestershire sauce	1 tsp.	5 mL
2. Green onion, sliced	1	1

1. Combine the first 4 ingredients in the bowl. Stir. Microwave, uncovered, on high (100%) for 2 to 3 minutes. Stir well. Microwave, uncovered, on high (100%) for 30 seconds until the cheese is melted.

2. Sprinkle with the green onion. Makes 2 cups (500 mL).

For spicy nachos, add some chilies. Use one or both of the cheeses. Do not freeze.

Nachos

GET READY ✔

baking sheet, dry measures, oven mitts, wire rack

1.	**Tortilla chips**	**2 oz.**	**57 g**
2.	**Grated Cheddar cheese**	**⅓ cup**	**75 mL**
	Grated Monterey Jack cheese	**⅓ cup**	**75 mL**
	Green onion, thinly sliced	**1**	**1**
	Green or ripe olives, sliced	**4**	**4**
3.	**Salsa**	**¼ cup**	**60 mL**
	Sour cream	**¼ cup**	**60 mL**

1. Place the oven rack in the center position. Turn the oven on to 350°F (175°C). Crowd the tortilla chips on the ungreased baking sheet.

2. Sprinkle with both cheeses, green onion and olive slices. Bake in the oven for about 3 minutes until the cheeses are melted. Use the oven mitts to remove the baking sheet to the wire rack.

3. Serve with the salsa and sour cream on the side. Serves 1.

Jiffy Pizza

GET READY ✔

frying pan, paper towel, sharp knife, cutting board, measuring spoons, small cup, small mixing spoon, baking sheet, table knife, oven mitts, wire rack

1.	Bacon slices	2	2
2.	Ketchup	2 tbsp.	30 mL
	Dried whole oregano	¼ tsp.	1 mL
	Onion powder	¼ tsp.	1 mL
3.	Hamburger bun, split and buttered	1	1
4.	Yellow cheese slices	2	2
	Mozzarella cheese slices	2	2

1. Place the oven rack in the top position. Turn the oven on to broil. Fry the bacon in the frying pan on medium-low until cooked but not crisp. Drain on the paper towel. Cut the slices into small pieces on the cutting board.

2. Stir the ketchup, oregano and onion powder in the small cup.

3. Place the 2 bun halves on the baking sheet. Spread the ketchup mixture with the table knife over the 2 bun halves.

4. Lay the cheese slices over the ketchup mixture. Sprinkle the bacon on the cheese. Broil in the oven for 1 to 2 minutes until the cheeses are melted. Watch carefully so that they don't burn. Use the oven mitts to remove the baking sheet to the wire rack. Serves 1.

A good quick pizza snack.

The next best thing to visiting Hawaii.

Hawaiian Grilled Cheese

GET READY ✔

non-stick frying pan, measuring spoons, table knife, pancake lifter, small plate

1.			
Margarine	2 tsp.	10 mL
White (or whole wheat) bread slices	2	2
Yellow cheese slices	2	2
Ham slice (1 oz., 28 g)	1	1
Pineapple slice, blotted very dry with paper towel	1	1

1. Heat the frying pan on medium-low. Spread the margarine on 1 side of each bread slice. Place 1 slice of cheese on the unbuttered side of each slice. Layer the ham and pineapple. Place the second slice of bread, buttered side up, on top. Set the sandwich in the frying pan. When the bottom side is browned, use the pancake lifter to turn the sandwich over. Brown the other side. Use the lifter to remove the sandwich to the plate. Makes 1 sandwich.

Pita Pizza

GET READY ✔
baking sheet, measuring spoons, dry measures, oven mitts, wire rack

1.	Pita bread (8 inch, 20 cm, size)	1	1
2.	Pizza (or spaghetti) sauce	2 tbsp.	30 mL
3.	Chopped cooked ham	2 tbsp.	30 mL
	Whole fresh mushrooms, chopped	2	2
	Grated mozzarella cheese	⅓ cup	75 mL
	Diced green pepper	2 tbsp.	30 mL

1. Place the oven rack in the top position. Turn the oven on to broil. Place the pita bread on the ungreased baking sheet. Flatten with your hand.

2. Spread the pizza sauce over the pita almost to the edge, using the back of the measuring spoon.

3. Sprinkle the ham, mushrooms, cheese and green pepper over the sauce. Broil in the oven for about 7 minutes until the cheese is melted and the edge of the pita is crisp. Use the oven mitts to remove the baking sheet to the wire rack to cool. Cuts into 6 wedges.

If you like a thin-crust pizza this is the one for you.

Pizza Pop-Ups

GET READY ✔
muffin pan (for 10 muffins), liquid measures, dry measures, measuring spoons, medium bowl, mixing spoon, oven mitts, wire rack

1.	Tomato sauce	½ cup	125 mL
	Chopped pepperoni	1 cup	250 mL
	Finely chopped onion	1 tbsp.	15 mL
	Grated Parmesan cheese	1 tbsp.	15 mL
	Grated mozzarella cheese	½ cup	125 mL
2.	Refrigerator flaky rolls (10 per tube)	12 oz.	340 g

1. Place the oven rack in the center position. Turn the oven on to 350°F (175°C). Grease the muffin pan. Mix the first 5 ingredients in the bowl.

2. Divide each roll in half. Place 1 piece of the dough in the bottom of each of the 10 muffin cups. Push down with your finger to form a shell. If the dough sticks to your finger, coat your finger with flour. Divide the pepperoni mixture among the 10 shells. Slightly flatten the remaining 10 pieces of the dough. Place over the pepperoni mixture. Push the edges down to seal. Bake in the oven for 15 to 20 minutes until golden. Use the oven mitts to remove the pan to the wire rack to cool. Makes 10 pop-ups.

Perfect for after basketball practice or video movie night.

These have a great nacho kick to them.

Nacho Potato Chunks

GET READY ✔
9 x 9 inch (22 x 22 cm) square baking pan, sharp knife, cutting board, small bowl, measuring spoons, mixing spoon, oven mitts, wire rack

1.	Unpeeled medium potatoes	2	2
2.	Cooking oil	1 tbsp.	15 mL
	Taco seasoning mix (from envelope)	2 tbsp.	30 mL
	Sour cream, for dipping		

1. Place the oven rack in the center position. Turn the oven on to 450°F (230°C). Grease the pan. Slice the potatoes in half lengthwise on the cutting board. Slice each half crosswise into 4 pieces to make 8 chunks for each potato. Place in the bowl.

2. Drizzle the cooking oil over the potato chunks. Sprinkle with the taco seasoning. Stir to coat well. Spread the potato in a single layer in the pan. Bake in the oven for 15 minutes. Use the oven mitts to remove the pan to the wire rack. Turn down the oven temperature to 400°F (205°C). Stir the potato chunks. Spread out. Bake for 15 minutes. Use the oven mitts to remove the pan to the wire rack to cool. Serve with the sour cream. Serves 2.

Variation: Sprinkle with ½ cup (125 mL) grated Cheddar or Monterey Jack cheese before the last baking time.

Serve with hamburgers
or on its own as a meal.
Do not freeze.

Taco Salad

GET READY ✔
dry measures, large bowl, small spoon, sharp knife, cutting board, liquid measures, measuring spoons, small bowl, small mixing spoon, pair of salad tongs (or 2 spoons)

1.	Chopped iceberg lettuce	4 cups	1 L
	Grated Cheddar cheese	1 cup	250 mL
	Can of kidney beans, drained	14 oz.	398 mL
	Large tomato, halved	1	1
	Green onions, sliced	4	4
2.	Tortilla chips, broken up	8 oz.	225 g
3.	Salad dressing (or mayonnaise)	½ cup	125 mL
	Taco seasoning mix (from envelope)	2 tbsp.	30 mL

1. Put the lettuce, cheese and kidney beans into the large bowl. Squeeze each tomato half to remove the juice. Use the small spoon to remove the seeds. Discard the juice and seeds. Dice the tomato on the cutting board. Add the tomato and green onion to the lettuce mixture.

2. Add the tortilla chips just before serving. If added too soon they will get soggy.

3. Stir the salad dressing and taco seasoning in the small bowl. Pour over the salad. Use the salad tongs to toss and coat the lettuce mixture with the dressing. Makes 8 side salads.

Almost like the adult version but so quick and easy. Make it for the whole family. Do not freeze.

Caesar Salad

GET READY ✔
measuring spoons, small bowl, mixing spoon, large bowl, dry measures, pair of salad tongs (or 2 spoons)

1. **DRESSING**

White vinegar	2 tbsp.	30 mL
Water	2 tbsp.	30 mL
Cooking oil	2 tsp.	10 mL
Granulated sugar	2 tsp.	10 mL
Prepared mustard	½ tsp.	2 mL
Garlic powder	¼ tsp.	1 mL

2.

Head of romaine lettuce	1	1
Croutons	1½ cups	375 mL
Grated Parmesan cheese	½ cup	125 mL
Large hard-boiled eggs, chopped	2	2

1. **Dressing:** Combine the first 6 ingredients in the small bowl. Stir well.

2. Wash and dry the lettuce. Tear into bite-size pieces. Put the lettuce into the large bowl. Add the croutons, cheese and egg. Pour the dressing over the lettuce mixture. Use the salad tongs to toss and coat the lettuce with the dressing. Serves 6.

Coconut Marshmallow Salad

GET READY ✔

dry measures, large bowl, mixing spoon, rubber spatula, plastic wrap

1.			
Miniature colored marshmallows	1 cup	250 mL
Can of fruit cocktail, well drained	14 oz.	398 mL
Can of mandarin oranges, well drained	10 oz.	284 mL
Long thread white or colored coconut (optional)	½ cup	125 mL
Maraschino cherries, halved	6	6
2. Sour cream (or plain yogurt)	1 cup	250 mL

1. Combine the marshmallows, drained fruits, coconut and cherries in the bowl. Stir.

2. Fold in the sour cream using the spatula. Cover the bowl with plastic wrap. Chill for 30 minutes to allow the flavors to blend and the marshmallows to soften. Makes 4 cups (1 L).

A showy rainbow of color.

Cottage cheese and peaches served on a bed of crisp lettuce.

Peaches 'N' Cream Salad

GET READY ✔
salad bowl (or salad plate), dry measures, small spoon, measuring spoons

1.	**Shredded crisp iceberg lettuce (handful)**		
2.	**Creamed cottage cheese**	½ cup	125 mL
3.	**Can of sliced peaches, juice reserved**	14 oz.	398 mL
	Reserved peach juice	1 tbsp.	15 mL
	Maraschino cherry, for garnish	1	1

1. Put the lettuce into the bowl or onto the plate.

2. Spoon the cottage cheese into the middle of the bed of lettuce.

3. Arrange the peach slices around the cottage cheese. Drizzle the peach juice over all. Top with the cherry. Serves 1.

FRUIT 'N' CREAM SALAD: Use canned fruit cocktail instead of the peaches.

JAM 'N' CREAM SALAD: Use 1 tbsp. (15 mL) jam on top if you don't have any fruit.

Apple Grape Salad

GET READY ✔

dry measures, medium bowl, 2 mixing spoons, measuring spoons, small bowl

1.	Red or green seedless grapes, halved	10	10
	Chopped walnuts (optional)	¼ cup	60 mL
	Thinly sliced celery	¼ cup	60 mL
	Small apple, cored and chopped	1	1
2.	Salad dressing (or mayonnaise)	2 tbsp.	30 mL
	Granulated sugar	1 tsp.	5 mL
	Lemon juice	1 tsp.	5 mL

1. Mix the first 4 ingredients in the medium bowl.

2. Stir the remaining 3 ingredients in the small bowl. Pour over the fruit mixture. Toss to coat. Makes 1½ cups (375 mL).

Crunchy but not too sweet. You'll give this a thumbs up!

For kids of all
ages. Tasty. Do
not freeze.

Carrot Raisin Salad

GET READY ✔
dry measures, medium bowl, mixing spoon, liquid measures, measuring spoons,
small bowl

1.	Grated carrot (2-3 medium)	2 cups	500 mL
	Raisins	½ cup	125 mL
	Canned crushed pineapple, drained	½ cup	125 mL
2.	Salad dressing (or mayonnaise)	⅓ cup	75 mL
	White vinegar	2 tsp.	10 mL
	Granulated sugar	2 tsp.	10 mL

1. Combine the carrot, raisins and pineapple in the medium bowl. Stir.

2. Measure the salad dressing, vinegar and sugar into the small bowl. Stir. Pour
   over the carrot mixture. Stir to coat. Makes about 2 cups (500 mL).

This delicious chowder is made from canned cream-style corn.

Corn Chowder

GET READY ✔
medium saucepan, dry measures, measuring spoons, liquid measures, 2 mixing spoons, hot pad

1.	Bacon slices, diced	2	2
2.	Chopped onion	¼ cup	60 mL
	Chopped green or red pepper	¼ cup	60 mL
	All-purpose flour	1 tbsp.	15 mL
	Milk	1 cup	250 mL
	Can of cream-style corn	14 oz.	398 mL
3.	Parsley flakes	1 tsp.	5 mL
	Hot pepper sauce, dash		
	Pepper, sprinkle		

1. Fry the bacon in the saucepan on medium until crisp. Do not drain.

2. Add the onion and green pepper. Sauté for 2 minutes until soft. Sprinkle the flour over the vegetables. Stir well. Slowly add the milk and corn, stirring constantly, until the mixture comes to a simmer. Remove the saucepan to the hot pad.

3. Add the remaining 3 ingredients. Stir. Makes 3 cups (750 mL).

Easy Macaroni Soup

GET READY ✔

liquid measures, measuring spoons, large saucepan, mixing spoon, dry measures, small bowl

1.	Water	4 cups	1 L
	Seasoned salt	½ tsp.	2 mL
	Package of macaroni and cheese dinner, cheese-flavored packet reserved	6½ oz.	200 g
2.	Frozen mixed vegetables	1 cup	250 mL
	Condensed chicken broth	10 oz.	284 mL
	Onion powder	1 tsp.	5 mL
	Pepper, sprinkle		
3.	All-purpose flour	2 tbsp.	30 mL
	Reserved cheese-flavored packet		
	Milk	1 cup	250 mL

1. Bring the water and seasoned salt to a boil in the saucepan. Add only the macaroni from the package. Boil for 5 minutes, stirring occasionally.

2. Add the vegetables, chicken broth, onion powder and pepper. Return to a boil. Cook for 5 minutes until the macaroni is tender.

3. Combine the flour and cheese-flavored packet in the bowl. Slowly add the milk, stirring constantly, until smooth. Add to the macaroni and vegetables in the saucepan. Cook, stirring constantly, for 2 or 3 minutes until heated through. Makes 7 cups (1.75 L).

If you like macaroni and cheese, you will want to try this recipe.

Easy to assemble and cook.

Chicken Barley Soup

GET READY ✔
liquid measures, measuring spoons, dry measures, large saucepan, mixing spoon, hot pad

1.	Water	5 cups	1.25 L
	Chicken bouillon powder	5 tsp.	25 mL
	Diced carrot	½ cup	125 mL
	Diced potato	½ cup	125 mL
	Diced onion	½ cup	125 mL
	Pearl barley	½ cup	125 mL
	Can of tomatoes, with juice, broken up	14 oz.	398 mL
2.	Can of flaked chicken (or turkey)	6½ oz.	184 g

1. Combine the first 7 ingredients in the saucepan. Stir. Heat on medium-high, stirring often, until the mixture comes to a boil. Place the lid on the saucepan. Turn down the heat to medium-low. Simmer, stirring occasionally, for about 1 hour.

2. Add the chicken. Simmer to heat through. Remove the saucepan to the hot pad. Makes 6½ cups (1.6 L).

Bean 'N' Bacon Soup

GET READY ✔
large saucepan, long-handled mixing spoon, colander, liquid measures, measuring spoons, hot pad

1.	Bacon slices, diced	2	2
	Small onion, chopped	1	1
2.	Large potato, diced	1	1
	Water	2 cups	500 mL
3.	Condensed vegetable soup	10 oz.	284 mL
	Can of beans in tomato sauce, mashed with a fork	14 oz.	398 mL
	Hot pepper sauce, dash	⅛-¼ tsp.	0.5-1 mL
4.	Grated Cheddar cheese, for garnish		

1. Fry the bacon in the saucepan on medium for 2 minutes. Add the onion. Stir. Sauté for about 5 minutes until the bacon is cooked and the onion is soft. Drain in the colander.

2. Add the potato and water. Bring the mixture to a boil. Place the lid on the saucepan. Simmer for 10 to 12 minutes until the potato is tender.

3. Add the vegetable soup, beans and hot pepper sauce. Simmer, uncovered, for 10 minutes. Stir occasionally. Remove the saucepan to the hot pad.

4. Garnish individual servings with the cheese. Makes 5½ cups (1.4 L).

Add more hot pepper sauce to make as zippy as you want.

You'll have fun making these. You can change the flavor of these little peanut butter balls just by rolling them in a different coating.

Peanut Butter Candy

 GET READY ✓
dry measures, medium bowl, measuring spoons, mixing spoon, small bowl, covered container

1.	Smooth or crunchy peanut butter	²/₃ cup	150 mL
	Granola cereal	³/₄ cup	175 mL
	Skim milk powder	¹/₃ cup	75 mL
	Brown sugar, packed	1 tbsp.	15 mL
2.	Mini semisweet or multi-colored chocolate baking chips	½ cup	125 mL
3.	Graham cracker (or Oreo cookie) crumbs, chocolate sprinkles or fine coconut, for coating	½ cup	125 mL

1. Put the peanut butter into the medium bowl. Add the cereal, milk powder and brown sugar. Mix with your hands.

2. Add the chocolate chips. Mix well. Shape the dough into 1 inch (2.5 cm) balls.

3. Place your choice of coating in the small bowl. Roll the balls in the coating. Place in a covered container. Chill. Makes 28 balls.

Toasted Coconut Mallows

GET READY ✔
dry measures, 9 × 9 inch (22 × 22 cm) square baking pan, oven mitts, hot pad, mixing spoon, small bowl, liquid measures, large saucepan, long-handled barbecue fork, paper towel, waxed paper

1.	Medium coconut	1 cup	250 mL
2.	Water	4-6 cups	1-1.5 L
3.	Large white or colored marshmallows	30	30

1. Place the oven rack in the center position. Turn the oven on to 350°F (175°C). Spread the coconut in the ungreased pan in an even layer. Bake in the oven for 6 minutes, removing with the oven mitts to the hot pad every 2 minutes to stir, until golden. Cool. Transfer to the bowl.

2. Put the water into the saucepan. Bring to a boil. Turn down the heat to medium.

3. Use the barbecue fork to dip each marshmallow quickly into the boiling water. Dab the marshmallow on the paper towel. Remove the marshmallow from the fork. Roll in the coconut. Set on the waxed paper to firm. Makes 30 marshmallow treats.

Impress your friends with these.

Cone Cupcakes

GET READY ✔

dry measures, medium bowl, electric mixer, measuring spoons, small bowl, mixing spoon, liquid measures, large table spoon, baking sheet, wooden toothpick

1.	Hard margarine, softened	½ cup	125 mL
	Granulated sugar	1 cup	250 mL
	Large eggs	2	2
	Vanilla flavoring	1 tsp.	5 mL
2.	All-purpose flour	1¾ cups	425 mL
	Baking powder	2½ tsp.	12 mL
	Salt	¼ tsp.	1 mL
3.	Milk	⅔ cup	150 mL
4.	Flat-bottomed ice-cream cones	24	24

Make for your friends or even your parents. Ice with your favorite colored icing.

1. Place the oven rack in the center position. Turn the oven on to 375°F (190°C). Cream the margarine and sugar well in the medium bowl on medium with the mixer. Beat in the eggs, 1 at a time, on high. Mix in the vanilla flavoring.

2. Measure the flour, baking powder and salt into the small bowl. Stir.

3. Add the milk to the margarine mixture in 2 parts, alternately with the flour mixture in 3 parts, beginning and ending with the flour mixture.

4. Spoon the batter into the cones to within ½ inch (12 mm) of the top. Set the filled cones on the baking sheet. Bake in the oven for 15 to 20 minutes until the wooden toothpick inserted in the center of each cone comes out clean. Makes 24 cupcakes.

Just bursting with color. Kids will love it. Best eaten the same day it is made.

Popcorn Cake

GET READY ✔
dry measures, large heavy saucepan, long-handled mixing spoon, very large bowl, 10 inch (25 cm) tube pan

1.	**Hard margarine**	**1 cup**	**250 mL**
	Large marshmallows	**32**	**32**
2.	**Popped popcorn (about**	**16 cups**	**4 L**
	¾ cup, 175 mL, unpopped)		
3.	**Small gumdrops (no black)**	**1 cup**	**250 mL**
	Chocolate-covered peanuts	**1 cup**	**250 mL**
	Smarties (or other coated candy)	**1 cup**	**250 mL**

1. Melt the margarine and marshmallows in the saucepan on low, stirring often.

2. Put the popped popcorn into the bowl. Pour the hot marshmallow mixture over the top. Quickly stir before the mixture starts to harden.

3. Quickly add the remaining 3 ingredients. Mix well. Pack into the greased tube pan. Cool completely. Cuts into 12 wedges.

Snowballs

GET READY ✔
dry measures, large saucepan, liquid measures, measuring spoons, long-handled mixing spoon, hot pad, small bowl, waxed paper, covered container

1.			
	Hard margarine	½ cup	125 mL
	Chopped pitted dates	2 cups	500 mL
	Water	¼ cup	60 mL
	Ground cinnamon	⅛ tsp.	0.5 mL
2.	Chopped walnuts (or pecans), optional	½ cup	125 mL
	Granola cereal	½ cup	125 mL
	Crisp rice cereal	½ cup	125 mL
3.	Flake coconut	¾ cup	175 mL

Crunchy and sweet. Made with granola and crisp rice cereal.

1. Melt the margarine in the saucepan on medium. Add the dates, water and cinnamon. Stir. Heat until the mixture comes to a boil. Turn down the heat to low. Heat, stirring constantly, for 5 minutes until the mixture is thickened. Remove the saucepan to the hot pad. Cool for 10 minutes.

2. Add the walnuts, granola cereal and rice cereal. Mix well.

3. Put the coconut into the small bowl. Wet your hands with water. Shape the cereal mixture into 1 inch (2.5 cm) balls. Roll the balls in the coconut. Place on the waxed paper on the counter or chill in a covered container. Serve at room temperature or chilled. Makes 30 balls.

These would make a great treat on Easter Sunday.

Marshmallow Nests

GET READY ✔
dry measures, medium microwave-safe bowl, mixing spoon, table spoon, waxed paper

1.	Smooth peanut butter	1 cup	250 mL
	Semisweet chocolate chips	1 cup	250 mL
2.	Large shredded wheat cereal biscuits	6	6
	Miniature white or colored marshmallows	60	60

1. Put the peanut butter and chocolate chips into the bowl. Microwave, uncovered, on high (100%) for 1 minute. Stir. Microwave, uncovered, on high (100%) for 1 minute. Stir to melt the chocolate chips.

2. Crumble the wheat cereal biscuits into the chocolate mixture. Stir until well coated. Drop by spoonfuls onto the waxed paper. Push 3 marshmallows into the middle of each to form a "nest with its eggs." Cool completely. Makes 20 nests.

Apple Pockets

Sweet and a bit gooey inside. Freeze any extras.

GET READY ✔
two 8 inch (20 cm) round cake pans, measuring spoons, small bowl, mixing spoon, oven mitts, wire racks, dry measures, small sealable plastic bag, scissors

1.	Tubes of refrigerator crescent-style rolls (8½ oz., 235 g, each)	2	2
2.	Small apple, peeled, cored and finely diced	1	1
	Granulated sugar	2 tbsp.	30 mL
	Ground cinnamon	½ tsp.	2 mL
3.	Icing (confectioner's) sugar	½ cup	125 mL
	Vanilla flavoring	½ tsp.	2 mL
	Milk	1 tbsp.	15 mL

1. Place the oven rack in the center position. Turn the oven on to 375°F (190°C). Grease the cake pans. Open the crescent rolls and separate into 16 triangles.

2. Combine the next 3 ingredients in the bowl. Mix well. Drop a small spoonful of the apple mixture near the wide end of each triangle. Fold the long points toward the middle over the top of the filling. Pinch to seal. Fold over to the third point. Pinch to seal. Place, seam-side down, in each cake pan, 8 per pan. Bake in the oven for 12 minutes until golden. Use the oven mitts to remove the cake pans to the wire racks.

3. Combine the icing sugar, vanilla flavoring and milk in the plastic bag. Squeeze out the air. Seal. Squish the bag to mix the ingredients until smooth. Make a tiny cut across 1 corner with the scissors. Squeeze a zigzag pattern over each pastry. Makes 16 pockets.

Chili Fries

Just like the ones you get in a fast-food restaurant—only better!

GET READY ✔
non-stick frying pan, dry measures, long-handled mixing spoon, measuring spoons, liquid measures, baking sheet, oven mitts, wire rack

1.	Lean ground beef	1 lb.	454 g
	Chopped onion	1 cup	250 mL
	Finely chopped celery	2 cups	500 mL
2.	All-purpose flour	1 tbsp.	15 mL
	Can of kidney beans, drained	14 oz.	398 mL
	Seasoned salt	1 tsp.	5 mL
	Pepper	⅛ tsp.	0.5 mL
	Chili powder	1½ tsp.	7 mL
	Can of tomato sauce	7½ oz.	213 mL
	Ketchup	¼ cup	60 mL
3.	Frozen french fries	4 cups	1 L

1. Place the oven rack in the center position. Turn the oven on to 425°F (220°C). Scramble-fry the ground beef in the frying pan on medium for 3 minutes with the long-handled mixing spoon. Add the onion and celery. Scramble-fry until the beef is no longer pink and the onion is soft.

2. Sprinkle with the flour. Stir well. Add the next 6 ingredients. Mix well. Bring to a boil. Pour into the ungreased baking sheet.

3. Top with the french fries. Bake in the oven for 25 to 30 minutes. Use the oven mitts to remove the baking sheet to the wire rack. Serves 6.

Carrot Combo

GET READY ✔

liquid measures, medium saucepan, dry measures, measuring spoons, sharp knife, colander, hot pad, potato masher

1. **Water**

Sliced carrot	**3 cups**	**750 mL**
Cubed yellow turnip	**1 cup**	**250 mL**
Salt	**½ tsp.**	**2 mL**
Granulated sugar	**½ tsp.**	**2 mL**

1. Pour enough water into the saucepan to be 1 inch (2.5 cm) deep. Add the carrot, turnip, salt and sugar. Place the lid on the saucepan. Bring to a boil on medium-high. Turn down the heat to medium-low. Simmer for about 20 minutes until the knife can easily pierce the vegetables. Drain in the colander. Return to the saucepan. Set the saucepan on the hot pad. Mash well. Serves 4.

Pictured on page 69.

Saucy Corn

GET READY ✔

measuring spoons, medium saucepan, mixing spoon, liquid measures, hot pad

1.
Margarine	**2 tbsp.**	**30 mL**
All-purpose flour	**2 tbsp.**	**30 mL**
Salt	**½ tsp.**	**2 mL**
Pepper	**⅛ tsp.**	**0.5 mL**
Milk	**1 cup**	**250 mL**

2.
Can of kernel corn, drained	**12 oz.**	**341 mL**
Finely chopped green pepper	**1 tbsp.**	**15 mL**
Finely chopped pimiento	**1 tbsp.**	**15 mL**

1. Melt the margarine in the saucepan. Mix in the flour, salt and pepper. Add the milk. Stir until the mixture is boiling and thickened.

2. Add the remaining 3 ingredients. Stir to heat through. Remove the saucepan to the hot pad. Serves 4.

Pictured on page 69.

Creamy Peas

GET READY ✔
dry measures, liquid measures, measuring spoons, small saucepan, mixing spoon, colander, hot pad

1.	Frozen peas	2½ cups	625 mL
	Water	½ cup	125 mL
	Chicken bouillon powder	½ tsp.	2 mL
2.	Sour cream	¼ cup	60 mL
	Salt, sprinkle		
	Pepper, sprinkle		

1. Combine the frozen peas, water and bouillon powder in the saucepan. Stir. Place the lid on the saucepan. Bring to a boil on medium. Turn down the heat to medium-low. Simmer for 3 minutes. Drain well.

2. Add the sour cream, salt and pepper. Stir to coat the peas. Return the saucepan to the burner. Heat through on low. Remove the saucepan to the hot pad. Makes 4 servings.

Carrot Combo, shown at the top, is made with turnips and carrots. Saucy Corn, bottom left, will make a colorful addition to any meal. Creamy Peas, bottom right, are a snap to make.

Flavorful Rice

1.			
	Long grain white rice	1 cup	250 mL
	Chopped onion	½ cup	125 mL
	Chicken bouillon powder	1 tsp.	5 mL
	Water	2 cups	500 mL
	Salt	½ tsp.	2 mL
2.	Water	½ cup	125 mL
	Frozen peas	1 cup	250 mL

1. Combine the first 5 ingredients in the medium saucepan. Stir. Place the lid on the saucepan. Bring the mixture to a boil on medium-high. Stir. Turn down the heat to medium-low. Simmer for 15 minutes until the rice is tender and the water is absorbed. Do not lift the lid while the rice is cooking.

2. Measure the second amount of water and frozen peas into the small saucepan. Place the lid on the saucepan. Bring to a boil on medium-high. Turn down the heat to medium-low. Simmer for 3 minutes. Drain in the colander. Stir the peas into the rice. Serves 4.

This rice is easy to make.
The peas add a burst of color
to this flavorful rice.

Mushroom Swiss Potato

GET READY ✔
table fork, paper towel, oven mitts, cutting board, measuring spoons, frying pan, mixing spoon, hot pad, sharp knife, small microwave-safe bowl, table spoon

1.	Unpeeled large potato	1	1
2.	Margarine	2 tsp.	10 mL
	Large whole fresh mushrooms, sliced	4	4
3.	Garlic powder, sprinkle		
	Salt, sprinkle		
	Pepper, sprinkle		
4.	Process Swiss cheese slice, cut into pieces	1	1

1. Wash the potato well. Poke 3 or 4 times with the fork. Wrap in the paper towel. Microwave on high (100%) for 7 minutes. Use the oven mitts to remove the potato to the cutting board.

2. Melt the margarine in the frying pan on medium. Add the mushrooms. Sauté for 1 minute.

3. Add the next 3 ingredients. Sauté until the mushrooms are golden. Remove the frying pan to the hot pad.

4. Cut a large X in the top of the potato, about 1 inch (2.5 cm) deep. Push the bottom sides inward to open the X slightly. Place the potato on the plate. Lay the pieces of cheese in the X. Spoon the mushrooms over the top. Microwave on high (100%) for 30 seconds to melt the cheese. Makes 1 large stuffed potato.

A hearty stuffed potato that is quick to make and nutritious.

Broccoli-Sauced Potatoes

GET READY ✔
table fork, measuring spoons, sharp knife, oven mitts, cutting board, dry measures, liquid measures, medium saucepan, colander, small bowl, hot pad, mixing spoon, 8 medium plates

1.	Unpeeled medium potatoes	4	4
	Cooking oil	1 tsp.	5 mL
2.	Chopped fresh (or frozen) broccoli	2 cups	500 mL
	Water	½ cup	125 mL
3.	Margarine	2 tbsp.	30 mL
	Chopped onion	¼ cup	60 mL
	All-purpose flour	3 tbsp.	50 mL
	Milk	1 cup	250 mL
4.	Process Swiss cheese slices, cut into small pieces	4	4
	Ground nutmeg, sprinkle		
	Seasoned salt	½ tsp.	2 mL
	Pepper, sprinkle		

1. Place the oven rack in the center position. Turn the oven on to 425°F (220°C). Wash the potatoes well. Poke 3 or 4 times with the fork. Coat your hands with the cooking oil and rub the potatoes all over. Bake in the oven for 45 to 50 minutes until tender when pierced with the knife. Use the oven mitts to remove the potatoes to the cutting board.

2. Put the broccoli into the water in the saucepan. Bring to a boil on medium-high. Turn down the heat to medium-low. Place the lid on the saucepan. Simmer for 5 minutes until tender. Drain the broccoli well in the colander. Place the broccoli in the bowl. Set on the hot pad.

3. Melt the margarine in the same saucepan on medium. Sauté the onion until soft. Sprinkle the flour over the onion. Mix well. Gradually add the milk, stirring constantly, until the sauce is boiling and thickened.

4. Stir the cheese into the hot sauce. Add the nutmeg, seasoned salt and pepper. Stir until the cheese is melted. Add the broccoli. Stir. Cut the potatoes in half. Place on the plates. Fluff up the insides with the fork. Spoon about ¼ cup (60 mL) broccoli sauce over each potato half. Makes 8 stuffed potato halves.

A delicious way to make ordinary baked potatoes special. Thick and creamy broccoli sauce in every mouthful.

# Measurement Tables

Throughout this book measurements are given in Conventional and Metric measures. The tables below provide a quick reference for the standard measures, weights, temperatures, and sizes.

Spoons

Conventional Measure	Metric Standard Measure Millilitre (mL)
⅛ teaspoon (tsp.)	0.5 mL
¼ teaspoon (tsp.)	1 mL
½ teaspoon (tsp.)	2 mL
1 teaspoon (tsp.)	5 mL
2 teaspoons (tsp.)	10 mL
1 tablespoon (tbsp.)	15 mL

Cups

Conventional Measure	Metric Standard Measure Millilitre (mL)
¼ cup (4 tbsp.)	60 mL
⅓ cup (5 tbsp.)	75 mL
½ cup (8 tbsp.)	125 mL
⅔ cup (10 tbsp.)	150 mL
¾ cup (12 tbsp.)	175 mL
1 cup (16 tbsp.)	250 mL
4 cups	1000 mL(1 L)

Weights

Ounces (oz.)	Grams (g)
1 oz.	28 g
2 oz.	57 g
3 oz.	85 g
4 oz.	113 g
5 oz.	140 g
6 oz.	170 g
7 oz.	200 g
8 oz.	225 g
16 oz. (1 lb.)	454 g
32 oz. (2 lbs.)	900 g
35 oz. (2.2 lbs.)	1000 g (1 kg)

Oven Temperature

Fahrenheit (°F)	Celsius (°C)
175°	80°
200°	95°
225°	110°
250°	120°
275°	140°
300°	150°
325°	160°
350°	175°
375°	190°
400°	205°
425°	220°
450°	230°
475°	240°
500°	260°

Pans

Conventional Inches	Metric Centimetres
8x8 inch	20x20 cm
9x9 inch	22x22 cm
9x13 inch	22x33 cm
10x15 inch	25x38 cm
11x17 inch	28x43 cm
8x2 inch round	20x5 cm
9x2 inch round	22x5 cm
10x4½ inch tube	25x11 cm
8x4x3 inch loaf	20x10x7.5 cm
9x5x3 inch loaf	22x12.5x7.5 cm

Casseroles

Conventional Quart (qt.)	Metric Litre (L)
1 qt.	1 L
1½ qt.	1.5 L
2 qt.	2 L
2½ qt.	2.5 L
3 qt.	3 L
4 qt.	4 L

Feature Recipe from
After-School Snacks

Come home to After-School Snacks for lots of quick and easy solutions for those before-supper hunger pangs.

Vegetable Pizza

GET READY ✔
12 inch (30 cm) pizza pan, dry measures, liquid measures, small bowl, mixing spoon, table knife, measuring spoons

1.	Biscuit mix	1⅛ cups	280 mL
	Milk	¼ cup	60 mL
2.	Spaghetti sauce	¼ cup	60 mL
3.	Grated mozzarella cheese	1 cup	250 mL
	Chopped green pepper	2 tbsp.	30 mL
	Sliced fresh mushrooms	¼ cup	60 mL
	Finely chopped onion	2 tbsp.	30 mL
	Pitted ripe olives, sliced	5-6	5-6

1. Place the oven rack in the center position. Turn the oven on to 375°F (190°C). Grease the pizza pan. Mix the biscuit mix and milk in the bowl to make a soft dough. Press firmly on the pan with your hand. Bake in the oven for 15 minutes to partially cook.

2. Use the knife to spread the spaghetti sauce over the crust.

3. Sprinkle the cheese over the top. Sprinkle with the green pepper, mushrooms, onion and olives. Bake in the oven for about 15 minutes until the cheese has bubbled up through the toppings. Cuts into 6 wedges.

Index

 # Cook's Notes

_____

_____

_____

_____

_____

_____

_____

_____

_____

_____

_____

_____

_____

_____

_____

_____

_____

_____

_____

_____

_____

_____

_____

_____

_____

_____

_____

_____

_____

_____

_____

_____

_____

_____

_____

_____

_____